JEFF GORDON

SPORTS GREAT OSCAR DE LA HOYA
0-7660-1066-X/ Torres

SPORTS GREAT WAYNE GRETZKY
0-89490-757-3/ Rappoport

SPORTS GREAT KEN GRIFFEY, JR.
0-7660-1266-2/ Savage

SPORTS GREAT GRANT HILL
0-7660-1467-3/ Torres

SPORTS GREAT DEREK JETER
0-7660-1470-3/ Knapp

SPORTS GREAT MICHAEL JORDAN
0-89490-978-9/ Aaseng

SPORTS GREAT REBECCA LOBO
0-7660-1466-5/ Savage

SPORTS GREAT STEPHON MARBURY
0-7660-1265-4/ Savage

SPORTS GREAT JERRY RICE
0-89490-419-1/ Dickey

SPORTS GREAT PETE SAMPRAS
0-89490-756-5/ Sherrow

SPORTS GREAT TIGER WOODS
0-7660-1468-1/ Macnow

SPORTS GREAT JEFF GORDON

Glen Macnow

—SPORTS GREAT BOOKS—

Enslow Publishers, Inc.

40 Industrial Road
Box 398
Berkeley Heights, NJ 07922
USA

PO Box 38
Aldershot
Hants GU12 6BP
UK

http://www.enslow.com

*To Noah Graff: Be true to yourself, always strive to excel—
and don't drive like a maniac.*

Library of Congress Cataloging-in-Publication Data

Macnow, Glen.
Sports great Jeff Gordon / Glen Macnow.
p. cm. — (Sports great books)
Includes index.
ISBN 0-7660-1469-X
1. Gordon, Jeff, 1971- —Juvenile literature. 2. Automobile racing drivers—
United States—Biography—Juvenile literature. [1. Gordon, Jeff, 1971–
2. Automobile racing drivers.] I. Title. II. Series.
GV1032.G67 M33 2001
796.72'092—dc21
00-012218

Printed in the United States of America

10 9 8 7 6 5 4 3 2 1

To Our Readers: We have done our best to make sure all Internet addresses in this book were active and appropriate when we went to press. However, the author and the publisher have no control over and assume no liability for the material available on those Internet sites or on other Web sites they may link to. Any comments or suggestions can be sent by e-mail to comments@enslow.com or to the address on the back cover.

Illustration Credits: AP/Wide World Photos.

Cover Illustration: AP/Wide World Photos.

Contents

Chapter 1

New Kind of Superstar

Pass or crash?

That was the dilemma Jeff Gordon faced. He pushed his car within inches of the tail of fellow driver Rusty Wallace at the 1999 Daytona 500 stock car race. There were just ten laps to go in the race, one of the crown jewels of the NASCAR circuit. With a half-million dollars at stake, Wallace was not about to move over and let Jeff Gordon slide by.

No, Wallace tried to keep his souped-up Ford Taurus directly in Gordon's path. If he could box Gordon in, Wallace figured, he could win the race.

Wallace could do nothing about Gordon's gambling nature, however. And he could do nothing to keep a slow car rolling out of the pits from helping decide a race in which speeds can reach 200 miles per hour.

Wallace kept his eye on the rearview mirror, watching Gordon's Chevrolet Monte Carlo behind him. Meanwhile, up ahead, another car was coming out of the pit road. The pit is where drivers get their tires changed and gas tanks refilled. Ricky Rudd's Ford was getting up to speed in the lane used for exiting a pit stop. The lane is not an area for

THE DAYTONA 500

Jeff Gordon holds up a sign in the victory lane at the Daytona International Speedway.

drivers at their peak speeds, because there is a great danger that they will ram a slow driver from behind.

Gordon knew that he had just one chance to pass the leader. He swerved left, going into the warm-up lane. He saw Ricky Rudd slowly coming up to speed. He thought, "Oh, Ricky, I hope you see me coming because I'm coming real fast."

Rudd did see Gordon, and he steered slightly to the left. As the cars went into a turn, Gordon sneaked his car within feet of the track's concrete wall. He was able to slingshot past Rudd. Then he used Rudd much like one basketball player uses another as a pick. He accelerated to maximum speed and swerved in front of Wallace. He kept his foot on the gas pedal and, a few laps later, was the leader as the checkered flag came out, signaling the end of the race.

The risky pass gave Gordon another win in his brilliant young career. But it could have resulted in a fiery crash.

"A couple of people could have died in that one," Rusty Wallace said after the race. "That would have been the biggest fire in the world. But Jeff isn't afraid to take risks. I guess that's why he has won a few races."

Won a few races? That is putting it mildly.

Since bursting onto the stock car racing scene in 1993, Jeff Gordon has been a force the likes of which has not been seen in racing in a long time. Gordon won three championships in four years on racing's Winston Cup circuit. That's like winning as many World Series, Stanley Cups, or Super Bowls in the same span—only harder, since auto racing has no substitutes, and an error can get you killed.

By his twenty-eighth birthday, Gordon had won fourty-six NASCAR races. He was the youngest driver ever to reach that number. His first Winston Cup title in 1995 made him, at age twenty-four, the youngest driver to win

Jeff Gordon (24) crosses the finish line ahead of Dale Earnhardt (3) to capture the Daytona 500 on February 14, 1999.

the award since Bill Rexford won at age twenty-three in 1950. The Winston Cup title is achieved by having more top finishes than other drivers. His 13 victories in 1998 tied the one-year record held by Richard "The King" Petty, who is regarded as the Babe Ruth of auto racing.

That same year, Gordon won four races in a row, tying a NASCAR record. For three straight years—1996, 1997, and 1998—he won at least ten races. No other driver in history could match that feat.

"I'm just a kid," Gordon said. "It's just a big blur, how fast I've gotten to this level. I can't even remember some things."

But his fans remember. More than 6 million of them attended the thirty-four Winston Cup races in 1999. An additional 160 million watched on television. The No. 1 attraction was Jeff Gordon and his rainbow-colored Monte Carlo, which carries the number twenty-four.

The abbreviation NASCAR stands for National Association for Stock Car Auto Racing. Unlike the fancy race cars in the Grand Prix or Indy circuits that look like something out of *Star Wars*, NASCAR's autos look just like the sedans found on American roads. The difference, of course, is that they are painted in garish colors and covered with sponsor logos. And their engines are souped up enough to tear down the raceway at 200 miles per hour.

In recent years, stock car racing has become as hot as a piston under a front-runner's hood. Attendance for the thirty-four-race Winston Cup series averaged 160,000 per event in 1999. In TV ratings, NASCAR racing blows away every major sport but pro football. The number of people who call themselves auto racing fans rose more than 60 percent during the 1990s.

It is not hard to see why. Stock car racing offers two kinds of superstars. There are the cars, which are colorful modern mechanical wonders. And there are the drivers,

Confetti fills the air as Jeff Gordon celebrates his Daytona 500 victory in 1999.

with their colorful personalities. NASCAR offers its fans the chance to get close to its athletes. Fans are often able to mingle with the drivers and their crews.

Most of the other drivers are a decade or two older than Jeff Gordon. And many—if not most—appeal to older fans.

"Jeff is opposite of what fans expect a racer should be," said Humpy Wheeler, president of the company that runs many of NASCAR's tracks. "He's not a good old tobacco-chewing guy. He's not a roughneck. He's young and polished and handsome. He's sort of like Michael Jordan in being a guy who can appeal to people who haven't been racing fans. He's sort of like Muhammad Ali and Arnold Palmer that way, too."

Gordon wears a milk mustache in commercials. He is on Jay Leno's and David Letterman's late-night talk shows, and *People* magazine's list of the "50 Most Beautiful People." He does soda commercials just like Deion Sanders and Shaquille O'Neal. He and his wife, Brooke, a former model, are featured on toothpaste packages.

The success and fame are amazing. Even more amazing is how the young driver has handled the money, the fans, the hangers-on, everything. Imagine having everything you ever dreamed of by your twenty-fourth birthday. Or driving professionally before you are old enough to have a driver's license. Or sitting in your school homeroom, next to a kid with a T-shirt sporting your likeness.

Jeff Gordon has had all those things. By all accounts, he is still a normal guy. Even so, racing's brightest star has an unusual relationship with its fans.

He is loved. From the moment he gets to a track until the moment he leaves, he cannot take two steps without drawing big crowds. People want to touch him, be photographed with him, have him sign their hats, their shirts—even their children.

Gordon hoists the winner's trophy high into the air after winning the Daytona 500 in February, 1999.

He is hated. Some race fans see him as too pretty. He is rich. He wins often, and sometimes makes it look easy. He married a gorgeous woman. Some fans are jealous.

When Gordon steps onto the track in his logo-splattered uniforms, he gets the loudest cheers of any driver—and the loudest boos. Gordon has said that the heckling does not bother him.

"I'm glad the people are making noise," he said. "It's a whole lot better going up there and hearing some cheers and some boos than it is if nobody is saying anything at all."

He has a really fast car—actually, eleven cars. There are four or five different models engineered for different racetracks. Fifteen mechanics work full-time on Gordon's cars in a vast garage in Charlotte, North Carolina, where he now lives. His crew is known as the Rainbow Warriors, because their uniforms carry the colorful logo of Gordon's top sponsor, the DuPont Corporation.

Gordon is part of the Hendrick Motorsports Racing Team. The team is run by millionaire auto dealer Rick Hendrick. The team provides Gordon with his cars and his crew and pays all his costs. He also gets a $2 million annual salary. Gordon and Rick Hendrick split evenly the money he makes winning races. In the five seasons from 1995 to 1999, the total winnings came to more than $29 million.

"People say, 'Jeff's got the best car, the best crew chief, the best engine,' " Gordon said. "That's true. I'd be the first to admit I can't go out there and win if I don't have the best of everything. I've been very blessed that way."

He has been blessed with a great deal of support since his earliest days. And he has been blessed with a great deal of talent. That became obvious not long after Jeff Gordon learned how to walk.

Chapter 2

Kid Gordon

It is not unusual for a pro basketball or baseball star to begin playing the sport as a small child. Most pro hockey players lace up skates soon after they learn to walk. Obviously, it is different for race car drivers. Most of them have to wait until they're older before they can get behind the wheel. Yet Jeff Gordon could hardly read the signs by the road when he first started driving.

Jeff's stepfather—a big-time racing fan—bought him a quarter-midget racer when he was just five. The car was much like a go-cart, but with a closed cockpit and a motor similar to those that power lawn mowers. It allowed Jeff, as a kindergartner, to zip around tracks at 20 miles per hour. This was before the youngster had even learned to ride a bike.

From the start, Jeff was a better driver than the other kids. He was fearless, passing the other tiny cars as he skidded around curves. But he was also safe. That came from one of his stepdad's rules: Whenever Jeff bumped another car in a race, he was not allowed to take home a trophy, even if he finished first.

Jeff's mother, Carol, was not so keen on her tiny son's hobby. The speedy race cars scared her. She would have preferred that Jeff join Little League. But, she later said, "Jeff drove hurt only once. And that came when he fell and broke his nose at the baby-sitter's house."

Jeff was three when his mom married his stepfather, John Bickford, a successful businessman in Vallejo, California. He had been working hard since he was a teenager. He wanted Jeff to have more fun than he did as a kid. So, when Jeff showed an interest in racing cars, Bickford did everything he could to help the little boy's dreams come true. He outfitted Jeff in an official driving uniform—gloves, helmet, and all—just like the pros wore. He ordered 144 Jeff Gordon T-shirts to sell when his stepson was just seven. He challenged Jeff by putting him against increasingly tough competition. "Most kids in quarter-midgets race maybe twenty weekends a year," John Bickford said. "We raced fifty-two weekends a year, everywhere in the United States. We had eight or nine cars. We practiced two or three times a week. And Jeff loved every minute of it."

Jeff's parents also made sure he found time for other things. They said that if he performed poorly in school, he would not get to race. That never became an issue. And he was a big movie fan as a child. His favorites were the *Star Wars* films. In fact, sometimes when he raced, Jeff thought of himself as Luke Skywalker. The Force always seemed to be with him.

By age seven, Jeff was winning every race he entered. At eight, he won his first national title. At nine, he was beating seventeen-year-olds in go-carts. At eleven, he won each of the twenty-five races he entered. Racing fans were driving hundreds of miles to see the prodigy with the knack for speed and a surgeon's touch. They marveled at how he would stalk a competitor into a turn. Then he would slice downward into a space that was barely there, pulling ahead

Jeff Gordon began driving a quarter-midget racer when he was just five years old.

as the two cars roared into the straightaway. Folks said the kid was a magician out there.

For $25,000, Bickford and Jeff built a sprint car: 1,300 pounds with a 650- horsepower engine. But finding opponents to race against in California began to be a problem.

"All the other parents were saying Jeff was probably lying about his age. They said he was probably twenty and just real little," said John Bickford. "Nobody wanted to race us. That was fine. We moved up to the superstock class (a higher-horsepower go-cart). Now we were running against guys seventeen and older—unlimited age. We were still winning. And those guys were going, 'There's no little kid who's going to run with us! Get out of here!'"

Finding competition became a serious problem. So in 1986, when Jeff was fourteen, the family made a big decision. Bickford sold his business, and the family used the money to move from California to Indiana, where auto racing was more popular and there was no minimum-age requirement. Jeff could now race sprint cars against the best in the business—even if his opponents were twice his age.

His young age created some funny moments. Jeff Gordon was all of fourteen when he showed up at the offices of the Valvoline Motor Oil company in Indiana one day in 1986. A rookie on the circuit, Jeff politely asked to be given the same deal other racers were getting from the local Valvoline dealers—free motor oil.

An amused executive asked young Jeff how he had gotten to the office.

"My mother drove me," Jeff replied.

"Now let me get this straight," the Valvoline man said. "You drive a 650-horsepower sprint car on half-mile tracks and you had to get your mom to drive you down here?"

Gordon was winning every race he entered by the age of seven years old. He won his first national racing title by age eight.

"Yes sir," Jeff said. "I'm not old enough to have a driver's license."

Needless to say, the oil man was impressed enough to give Jeff Gordon the deal. It was the first time—but not the last—that Jeff showed himself to be a shrewd businessman.

At age sixteen, Jeff was beating the best racers in the area. Some were twice his age. Some auto racing fans predicted he would be the next great driver, following legends like Richard Petty, Cale Yarborough, and Darrell Waltrip. This was Jeff's dream.

There was disagreement in Jeff's family, though. His parents both wanted him to go to college, to experience new things and learn other subjects. After that, if Jeff still wanted to go into racing, at least he would have something to fall back on. For most of Jeff's senior year of high school, he and his parents debated his future. Finally they made a deal: If Jeff raced well the summer after high school, he could continue racing. If not, he would go to college.

There is a turning point in the lives of most sport stars. For Jeff Gordon it came on the day of his high school graduation. On that same day, a big race featuring some of the top drivers in the region was held near Jeff's home at a dirt track in Bloomington, Indiana. In his mind, it meant that the big boys were coming to town. They were coming into his territory. He desperately wanted to be in the race.

Jeff's parents told him he had to attend graduation. He looked at the schedules. The ceremony would end before the qualifying race began. So Jeff got his diploma with his classmates, and then drove to the racetrack in his cap and gown. He made it just in time. He finished fourth in qualifying and second in the feature race against some of the world's best drivers.

"I was just beaming," he said later. "That was one of

the best days of my life." After that race, his parents allowed him to put off college to pursue his racing career.

He still had one important decision to make. Jeff had never raced in a full-sized car. Just as he had graduated from high school, he had to graduate to the next level on the racing circuit.

Auto racing is divided into several categories. Stock cars resemble cars you would find on the street, except that they have souped-up engines. Indy cars are specially designed high-performance cars that zip around at 225 miles per hour. Formula One cars are smaller than the other two, and they usually run in races that wind through city streets.

Gordon toyed with each possibility. He decided against Grand Prix, because it is more popular in Europe than in the United States. He considered the Indy car circuit, but was told that it is difficult for young stars to break in. He decided to attend a stock car driving school in North Carolina run by former NASCAR star Buck Baker.

Gordon climbed into a stock car for the first time. "This is it," he said to himself. "This is what I want to do. . . . The car was different from anything that I was used to. . . . It was so big and heavy. It felt very fast but very smooth. I loved it."

He finished stock car school as the star pupil. In 1991 he joined NASCAR's Busch Series, which is stock car racing's equivalent to a baseball minor league. He won several races and was named the circuit's Rookie of the Year.

Jeff now felt he was ready for the big time—NASCAR's Winston Cup circuit. All he needed was a sponsor. Auto racing is a tremendously expensive sport. Each driver requires cars and equipment totaling more than $1 million. In addition, each driver needs a pit crew, an engineer, and several mechanics. In the big business of NASCAR, no

By the time he was sixteen, Jeff Gordon was regularly beating drivers twice his age. Many predicted he would be racing's next great performer.

driver can survive without a sponsor willing to pick up the expenses.

Gordon was a hotshot rookie. Finding a sponsor would not be difficult. Still, Jeff wanted the right car owner—someone who would care as much about him as a person as about the amount of money he won. He met such an owner on March 10, 1992.

Rick Hendrick, who owns the biggest team in racing, was at a Busch race in Atlanta that day. Out of the corner of his eye, he spotted a white car accelerating through a turn.

"Man, that guy's gonna wreck!" Hendrick shouted. "You can't drive a car that loose."

Veteran drivers Dale Earnhardt and Harry Gant were being passed by the kid in the white car. Hendrick asked who the driver was and was told, "That's the kid, Gordon."

Hendrick scratched his chin and pondered his future. Soon a great partnership would be born.

Chapter 3

Wonder Boy

Just a few days after that 1992 race, Rick Hendrick agreed to be Jeff Gordon's car owner. In NASCAR racing, each driver needs an owner to pay for everything from new engines to plane flights to the next event. In return, the owner gets a share of the driver's prize winnings. Hendrick is a multimillionaire. His three racing teams can afford the best of everything.

"Jeff had it all," Hendrick said after their first meeting. "It was just scary. He's good-looking, and I couldn't believe how well he handled himself at age twenty. What I found was a mature young guy who was kind of humble—a little bashful. A sponsor's dream."

Gordon started on the NASCAR Busch Series Grand National Division, a good training circuit. Late in 1992 he made his NASCAR Winston Cup Series debut at Atlanta. He finished thirty-first among forty-one drivers.

By 1993 he was ready for the big time. Gordon made a splash by becoming, at twenty-one, the youngest driver ever to win a 125-mile qualifying race for the Daytona 500. The victory was nice, but by that time Gordon had already won more than six hundred races in various types of cars. Gordon entered thirty races in 1993. He did not win any, but he had seven top-five finishes. He earned $765,000 and was named Winston Cup Rookie of the Year. He also wrecked a lot of cars. Veteran drivers criticized him for careless driving. Unlike many young athletes, Gordon listened to his older critics.

"These guys want to lead you down a path and teach you just like a parent does," he said. "They know by helping you out it's only going to help the sport. So now I'm starting to ask more questions. There are many things I can learn from Darrell Waltrip or Dale Earnhardt or whoever has been in the sport for a while."

Well, he learned fast. Gordon notched his first career win at Charlotte, in the 1994 Coca-Cola 600. A month later, back in his adopted home state of Indiana, he won the first-ever Brickyard 400, held at historic Indianapolis Motor Speedway. For the first three-quarters of the race, he ran in the shadow of Bill Elliott's Ford Taurus. Then, with just a few laps to go, Gordon zipped his multicolored Chevy past Elliott and rode to a dramatic victory. He ended the season ranked eighth among drivers and with earnings of $1.6 million.

Still he was not satisfied. Being the world's eighth-best driver was not good enough. Gordon raised some eyebrows after that season when he declared his plan to run for the title in 1995. After all, he was just twenty-two years old. Just one driver in NASCAR history—Richard Petty—had finished first at so young an age.

Gordon also raised eyebrows late in 1994 by marrying Brooke Sealey, a model who held the title of Miss Winston Cup. The two met in Victory Lane at Daytona in 1993. They discovered that they shared deep religious beliefs—and a love of ice cream. Because Winston Cup models are not allowed to date drivers, they began meeting secretly. When they got engaged a year later, almost no one on the circuit knew they had been seeing each other. Today, Jeff and Brooke Gordon live in North Carolina. When they can

Winston Cup Rookie of the Year Jeff Gordon (left) stands alongside NASCAR Winston Cup Champion Dale Earnhardt during a news conference on December 2, 1993.

manage spare time, they take skiing vacations—on both water and snow. One room of their house is filled with video games and pinball machines. Those are Gordon's escape from his pressure-packed job.

There was no question that Gordon was the fastest-rising star in NASCAR as the 1995 season opened. The question was, how fast and how high could he rise? No one, except perhaps Gordon himself, could have foreseen his amazing success.

As of 2000, there were over forty-five drivers on the NASCAR Winston Cup circuit and just thirty-five events a year. Because there are fewer racers than there are drivers, a driver is beating the odds if he wins one race. A year with two wins is a great year. Five are almost unheard of.

As 1995 unfolded, Gordon was on a phenomenal roll. By the end of March he already had three victories—in Rockingham, North Carolina; Atlanta, Georgia; and Bristol, Tennessee. All were runaways. He was on his way toward another win, in Darlington, South Carolina, when he got caught up in a wreck caused by others. In early April, at North Wilkesboro, North Carolina, Gordon led for most of the race. A worn right rear tire left him second to Dale Earnhardt at the finish. Earnhardt admitted he was lucky to win.

A few weeks later, at the New Hampshire International Speedway, Gordon was running qualifying laps for the Slick 50 300. The men operating stopwatches by the side of the track shook their heads in disbelief as Gordon's speeds approached 200 miles per hour. Then the worst happened. Gordon spun on an oil slick, and two of his wheels made contact with an outside wall. The wall swallowed up the side and rear of Gordon's Chevrolet destroying it in one big gulp.

Gordon got out. He was not hurt, but sitting before him were 3,400 pounds of damaged race car. With the race

Gordon celebrates with his wife Brooke after winning the DieHard 500 in April 2000. The two first met in 1993 and were married in 1994.

taking place the next day, Gordon feared he was out of the contest.

His team of mechanics and repairmen was not ready to give up. The Rainbow Warriors worked all night to replace the rear end, deck lid, right quarter panel, and right front. By noon the next day, the crumpled sheet metal was only a distant memory. Fresh paint covered the car.

"I was amazed that my team could save the car," Gordon said. "I figured I owed them one for that. I had to pay them back for their effort."

Because of the crash, Gordon started the race from the twenty-first position. That is far from the front, and gives the driver a lot of distance to make up. Halfway through the three-hundred-lap race, Gordon had climbed to fourth place. Dale Earnhardt and Rusty Wallace battled side by side, while Ricky Rudd enjoyed the show from behind them.

Wallace was forced to back out of the pack on Lap 164 when he and Rudd bumped, causing Wallace's fender to rub on his own left front tire. After a stop to pull the sheet metal away, Wallace found himself in nineteenth place and out of contention.

Earnhardt fell from contention during a pit stop when loose lug nuts were discovered during on his car. It took a while to replace them, causing his Chevrolet to fall back to twenty-second, a lap down.

Now only Rudd's black-and-yellow Ford stood between Gordon and another victory. With twenty-five laps left, Rudd skidded high into a corner during a turn. Gordon sensed the tiny opening. He slipped in low, and zoomed past Rudd coming out of the turn. In the last few miles, Gordon opened the lead. He won by just over a second.

The wins just kept on coming. When the NASCAR season ended in November, Gordon had run in thirty-one races. He had won 7 of them, a tremendous deed. He finished in the top five in ten other races, and finished in the top ten another six times.

There were two other important numbers. Gordon's total winnings from the thirty-one races came close to $4.4 million. No other driver in NASCAR history had ever topped $4 million in a year. Also, NASCAR's scoring system for its drivers awards points based on each finish. At the end of 1995, Gordon—who had just turned twenty-four—took the points title away from Dale Earnhardt. Just as he had hoped before the season started, he was driving home the Winston Cup Trophy in his Chevy Monte Carlo.

Suddenly the likable kid was the reigning superstar of auto racing. In a span of less than one hundred Winston Cup races, Gordon had gone from rookie to champion. His nickname had evolved from Jeff Who? to The Kid, to Flash Gordon, and finally to Wonder Boy. His name was now mentioned alongside the all-time greats of the sport, men like Petty, Earnhardt, David Pearson, and Darrell Waltrip.

Sometimes easy success can take away a person's drive to strive even harder. Yet there was no reason to worry with Jeff Gordon. Even as he kept winning, he remained himself—polite, shy, and polished. How did the young man keep his head on straight? Gordon said the answer was not to think that he was living out his dreams (although he really was). The answer was to regard racing as his job.

"People say to me, 'You're supposed to race because you enjoy it, not because you're trying to make money,'" Gordon said. "But if I don't make it a job, then I'm not going to be serious enough about it. My job is to focus one hundred percent on winning. If I do my job, then the money and fun will follow. But I have to work at it like anyone else works at his career."

Still, he did allow himself the luxury of some fun. When the 1995 season ended, Jeff and Brooke flew to Hawaii for

Gordon holds up a bottle of champagne after clinching the Winston Cup Championship with his victory at the NAPA 500 at the Atlanta Motor Speedway in Hampton, Georgia, on November 12, 1995.

a vacation. They water-skied and jet-skied and searched for any other activity that involved speed. Then Jeff took another few weeks off just to answer the fan mail that had been stacking up. Letters came from Canada, France, England, Italy, Germany, Austria, Hungary, the Dominican Republic, every small town in America, and elsewhere. One found him with just the address "Jeff Gordon, U.S.A." on it.

Gordon was now among the world's most popular athletes. He was photographed for the covers of men's fashion magazines. He was asked to endorse everything from video games to bike helmets. He got thirty requests a week to make speeches.

"It's a good problem to have," Gordon said. "If people want me, that must mean they like me. The problem comes when people stop asking for your autograph."

No chance of that. But to stay in demand, Gordon knew, he had to show that 1995 was no fluke. Could he repeat his performance in 1996? Many experts doubted it. Yet Gordon was determined to do even better.

Chapter 4

On the Fast Track

Someone who does not follow NASCAR may think that auto racing does not require much athletic skill. After all, almost every adult drives. And how many kids look at their parents as athletes at the end of the daily car pool run?

Pushing a 3,500-pound stock car for over three hours requires strength, stamina, and cat-quick reflexes. Jeff Gordon stands five feet seven inches and weighs just 150 pounds. As he looked back on his great 1995 season, Gordon decided he could be even better if he could build up his strength.

He committed himself to a vigorous workout schedule. Four times a week, year round, Gordon makes time to do two hundred sit-ups and 150 push-ups. The other three days he runs a minimum of two miles, and as much as five miles. The only days off from the exercise are the days he races.

The dedication to fitness has made Gordon one of the most finely tuned athletes this side of Shaquille O'Neal. Gordon believes the exercise has kept him from ever falling into a long slump.

In 1996, Gordon won ten races. Under NASCAR's complicated points formula, he just missed repeating as season champ. He finished thirty-seven points behind Terry Labonte (4,657–4,620).

The season's highlight came in June at the Dover Downs International Speedway in Delaware. The track is a scary one, with sharp turns and concrete walls built close to the track. On this day there was a slight drizzle, which dampened the track.

Gordon led for most of the first 190 miles. Then, as Gordon was about to lap the field, Rick Mast's No. 14 Pontiac spun out in front of him. Using his quick reflexes, Gordon slammed on his brakes. He veered onto the road that drivers use before taking pit stops. He was out of danger, but as Gordon looked around, he saw Labonte, Dale Earnhardt, and others zoom past Mast's sliding car. Suddenly, Gordon was in fourteenth place, well back of leader Earnhardt.

Rather than panic, as some young drivers might, Gordon showed patience. "When you get behind those guys you can't let yourself get frustrated," he said after the race. "You can't try to run them down all at once. You really mess up your tires when you do that."

Gordon knew he had half the race left. So he started picking off the drivers in front of him—one by one. First he focused on John Andretti, who was in thirteenth place. When Andretti took a turn high, Gordon zipped underneath and passed him. A few car lengths ahead was Bobby Hamilton in twelfth. Gordon waited a few laps for Hamilton to get boxed in traffic, and then passed him.

Lap after lap, mile after mile, Gordon locked eyes on the man directly in front of him. Gradually his rainbow-colored Chevy crawled back into the race that he had been leading. When Earnhardt was forced to take a pit stop at mile 363, Gordon found himself back in the lead. From

Gordon (24) avoids Ricky Craven (41) as he flips into the catchfence during the Winston Select 500 in April 1996. Gordon's reflexes and his dedication to training have been key factors in his success on the track.

then on, he never looked back. When the checkered flag came out, he was far in front.

By the time the 1997 season started, Gordon was no longer regarded as the upstart kid. Veteran drivers had learned to respect him—mostly because he just kept on winning.

"I've seen all the greats," said Geoff Bodine, who has been driving on the NASCAR circuit since 1979. "I've raced against Richard Petty and Dale [Earnhardt]. Against David Pearson and Cale Yarborough. Usually found myself chasing their tails. Now it's Jeff's tail that I'm always chasing."

In fact, they all chased Gordon's tail in 1997. He won another 10 races, to lead the pack. He finished in the top five in twenty-six of his thirty-two starts. And he took home earnings of almost $6.4 million—a NASCAR record.

Beyond the mere statistics, Gordon won in spectacular fashion. At Bristol, he banged his DuPont Auto Finishes Chevy under the Ford of Rusty Wallace in the last corner, to grab the victory. At Martinsville, Gordon and Jimmy Spencer were vying for the lead when their cars came together. Both spun out. Gordon regained his composure first and drove on to victory.

Part of Gordon's success is his willingness to drive aggressively—although some of his competitors call him reckless. "I really feel like I learn a little bit more as a driver each race," he said. "Whether it's learning to be a little more patient or a little more aggressive. I just want to be a driver who never stops and never quits and gets 100 percent out of the race car at all times."

The highlight of the season came in February 1997, at one of the biggest races, the Daytona 500. Gordon was not just part of a win there. He was part of a one-two-three trifecta.

Although auto racing is an individual sport, all

Gordon takes the checkered flag as he wins the Miller 500 at the Dover Downs International Speedway in Dover, Delaware, on June 2, 1996.

NASCAR racers belong to teams. Gordon races for the Hendrick Driving Team, and he is not alone. Two other top drivers—Terry Labonte and Ricky Craven—are part of the Hendrick team. The Hendrick Boys, as they are known, are respected for having the best equipment and the smartest minds on the circuit.

During most of the 1997 season, team owner Rick Hendrick was hospitalized with a serious illness. Gordon dedicated his victories to his car owner. And what could be better than a Gordon victory? How about a one-two-three finish by the Hendrick teammates?

It happened at the Daytona 500. With just eleven of the two hundred laps left in the race, Gordon was trying to overtake Earnhardt for second place. Gordon charged low into Turn 2 and came back up into the middle of the track as he entered the straightaway. Earnhardt, however, stayed high coming out of the turn and scraped the retaining wall. Their two cars bumped together for an instant. Earnhardt lost control for a moment. An onrushing pair of former Daytona 500 winners, Dale Jarrett and Ernie Irvan, could not keep from ramming Earnhardt's car and flipping it. Suddenly it was rolling over and over down the backstretch. All three men—Earnhardt, Jarrett, and Irvan—found themselves out of the picture.

That left the three Hendrick Boys chasing race leader Bill Elliott to the finish. Elliott looked in his rearview mirror. "With three Hendrick cars behind you, you ain't got a chance," Elliott said when all was done. "I was dead meat, and I knew it. It was just a matter of when and where."

Gordon, too, realized the situation. Seeing Elliott in front of him and two teammates right behind him was "a sign. A good sign," he thought.

With six laps to go, the three teammates lined up. That created an enormous air blast that gave Gordon's car an extra jolt of energy. They sneaked up behind Elliott. Then they fanned out. As Elliott desperately tried to decide which car to block, all three sped past him. And that was that. When the checkered flag came out, it was Gordon first, Labonte second, and Craven third.

"It didn't matter which of us finished first, second or third," Gordon said afterward. "So long as we finished one-two-three for Rick." Never before had one team swept the top three spots in a NASCAR race.

So how could Gordon top his championship season in 1997? How about doing it again? That is exactly what he did in 1998—taking the NASCAR driving title for the third time in four years. This time he had 13 first-place finishes—tying the all-time single-season record. He won another $9.3 million dollars. That gave him 42 NASCAR wins and nearly $26 million in earnings shortly after his twenty-seventh birthday. Those are phenomenal numbers.

How good is Jeff Gordon? "He's so good that he should have to drive a Humvee in place of his Monte Carlo," said rival team owner Felix Sabates. "Or maybe he should have to drive on three wheels."

Gordon is helped by his great talent. He is helped by his great crew. And sometimes he is helped by a little bit of luck.

All three of those factors came together in Tennessee in 1998, in the Food City 500 at Bristol Motor Speedway. For the first four hundred or so miles, Gordon chased the leaders. But he could not find enough stamina in his car to catch up. Then a minor accident caused the racers to slow down for a few minutes. Gordon pulled into the pit, where his crew began tinkering with his engine. When the race was restarted, Gordon zoomed out of the pit. Suddenly his car seemed to have much more power. The few twists and turns on his engine by Gordon's crew seemed to add a

Gordon (24), Terry Labonte (5), and Ricky Craven (25) finish 1-2-3 at the 1997 Daytona 500. This was the first time one team swept the top three spots in a NASCAR race.

considerable amount of speed to his racer. That is where the crew's help came in.

Gordon passed a few drivers and set his sights on race leader Rusty Wallace. Then a freak accident took place. A piece of debris seemed to fall from Ricky Rudd's Ford. It bounced along the track until Wallace ran over it. The object cut Wallace's tire. It sent him bouncing into the retaining wall. He was out of the race. That is where luck—Wallace's bad luck and Gordon's good luck—came in.

Now Gordon had the lead. This was where his talent came in. He held off a few challenges and won. It was the fourth straight time he won the spring race at Bristol Motor Speedway.

Chapter 5

The Day of the Race

Ever wonder what it is like to drive a Winston Cup racer? Take a ride with Jeff Gordon.

Gordon's No. 24 Chevrolet Monte Carlo is painted in the colors of the rainbow. It is also covered with more than forty advertising logos. Fans say they go out of their way to buy the sponsors' products.

There are no doors on this car. To get in, the driver must climb through the window. A series of crisscross seat belts strap you into this powerful machine. If the five-point harness is not tight enough to hurt the driver's chest, it is not tight enough to be safe. To fight the 140-degree temperature that develops in the car during a race, Gordon flips on a fan that blows air straight into his helmet.

There is also no key for this car. To start it, the driver flips a series of toggle switches. The car starts with a deafening roar that may scare a first-timer.

Now the car is ready to drive, but there is far more to getting a stock car around the track than pressing the gas pedal and turning left. Long before the pit marshal waves the checkered flag signaling the start, an experienced racer will take note of conditions. On a summer afternoon, for example, a track's asphalt might be soft from the heat. That will lessen the grip of the tires. To warm up the tires, he swerves slightly from side to side during the first few miles.

The first laps of the race—the warm-up laps—are run slowly. A pace car sets the speed for the forty-three racers in the field. Now, as the laps end, the pace car pulls off the track. Another flag—a green flag—is about to wave, telling racers they can now drive as fast as they want. Gordon tries to time his move to beat the green flag by a split-second. That would give him a tiny edge on the rest of the field.

"I'm looking for that green flag," he says. "Just a little bit before it drops, just as he starts to wave it, I'm going."

Now the car begins to build up speed. It hits 100 miles per hour . . . then 125 . . . then 150. As the scenery begins to blur, you realize how bumpy the ride is. "Our cars are not built for comfort," Gordon says. "The difference between them and street cars is the stiffness of the springs and shock absorbers. When you hit a bump in a race car, it shocks you. But I want to feel the bumps so I know how the car's responding and I can react to it."

Concentration is a key as the driver approaches 200 miles per hour. An everyday driver may tool down the highway, listening to the radio, hardly thinking about what he is doing. Gordon has to pay much more attention. There is usually a guy on his bumper. Another guy tries to pass him on the left, and another on the right. Yet another is right in front of him, determined to keep him in his rearview mirror. They are all doing 200 miles per hour.

There is a sharp curve ahead. Everybody wants to get there first. Nobody is giving an inch. It is incredibly loud, and everyone's nerves are on edge. Any split-second decision might mean the difference between life and death.

"You're so focused," Gordon says. "Your mind is concentrating so much on getting that car to go as fast as you possibly can. At that speed, you're on the absolute

Jeff Gordon's No. 24 Chevrolet Monte Carlo is painted in a wide variety of colors and is covered with over forty advertising logos.

edge. The last thing you want to do is have your mind on anything else but driving that race car."

On long straightaways, however, Gordon talks and listens in his radio headset. He has members of his crew set up in three or four spots around the track. They tell him what lies up ahead. When is the perfect time to pass another driver? What dangers lurk in the next turn? What other racers are looking good today? When is he due for a pit stop?

The pit stop is often where a race car turns into a real winner. Auto races can be six hundred miles long and take five hours to complete. Sometimes the difference between first and second place is less than a second. The time spent servicing the car can often decide the winner. And Gordon's crew puts on an amazing display. In less than twenty seconds, a team of seven men changes four tires and fills the gas tank.

In a typical five-hundred-mile race, Gordon will go through twenty-four tires and one hundred gallons of gas. That usually means five pit stops—more if the car is having mechanical trouble.

The pit jobs are dangerous and must be performed exactly right. The two men who handle the gas wear special fireproof suits. Even a tiny spill of fuel on the hot car can start a fire.

The tire changers must work quickly. They use high-powered wrenches to remove the lug nuts holding on each tire. They hand the old tire to an assistant and replace it with a new one—all within seconds. A jammed or lost lug nut can ruin the driver's afternoon.

Everyone on the crew has a specific job. There is even someone whose job it is to clean the windshield and hand Gordon a cold drink.

All of this happens in less than twenty seconds—not bad timing. Now the race begins again.

Crew members leap into action as Gordon pulls in to the pit stop during the Dura-Lube/Big Kmart 400 in February, 1999. Many races are decided by the pit crews.

As Gordon shifts gears, his car's souped-up V-8 engine roars. He shifts into third gear, and then fourth. The car jumps as it approaches 200 miles per hour. Gordon slips into the middle of the pack of forty-three racers. That allows him to glide a bit on the wind created by those in front of him. On most days he does not make his move until midway through the race.

Today it begins on Lap 154 of the three-hundred-lap contest. Gordon spots Dale Earnhardt in his black No. 3 Chevy looming ahead. He tails Earnhardt for a full lap, until Earnhardt takes a wide turn in the backstretch. Gordon swiftly ducks inside his opponent and leaves Earnhardt in his dust.

With the race nearly two-thirds over, Gordon is stuck in seventh place. Is it time to panic? Not at all. Instead, Gordon looks at each driver ahead of him and figures his strategy—one car at a time.

He passes three just on sheer speed. Now he is chasing Rusty Wallace for third place. Gordon's crew radios him that Wallace's last pit stop was twenty laps earlier than his. That means Wallace's tires must be worn.

Gordon chases him, stays on him, and makes Wallace use up his tires. With seventeen laps to go, Gordon tucks in on Wallace's rear bumper. That move, combined with Wallace's tired tires, sends Wallace's Taurus high on the track. Gordon sees an opening and pounces. He passes Wallace on the outside to move into second. Then Wallace locks right back onto Gordon's bumper, turns the tables, and becomes the stalker.

"You want to get away from him," says Gordon. "Get as far away from him as you can, or he's going to get right back up on you and loosen you up and pass you. If he does that too late in a race, you're done."

Now, there are nine laps left in the long race. Most of the drivers are exhausted. For several hours, they have

Jeff Gordon triumphantly holds the Winston Cup trophy after winning the Winston Cup Championship for the third time in November, 1998.

been turning the steering wheel, shifting gears, keeping an eye on everything around them. Again, some people argue that race drivers are not athletes. Jeff Gordon disagrees. During a race, he often loses eight pounds. After a race, his eye muscles ache from the hours of concentration. He is so intense when driving that, he says, "someone could shoot me and I probably wouldn't notice."

And there is one other physical challenge. Some auto races last as long as four or five hours. Drivers get no bathroom break. How does he do it?

"It really is amazing how mind over matter works. I can remember times when it was real hot and I'm drinking a lot of fluids. Then I'm in the car buckling up and I say, 'Oh, no! I have to go right now. How am I going to make it the whole race?' But I make it. And an hour after the race I'll remember, 'Oh, yeah. I have to go to the bathroom.'"

Certainly, that is not on his mind now. With just a few laps left, he finds himself hanging on to the back bumper of Ernie Irvan's black Ford Taurus. Gordon waits for a long straightaway, and pulls up outside Irvan.

With four laps to go, the two men roar through the turns side by side. Gordon thinks to himself, "The last guy I want to race at the end is Ernie. He's smart and he never makes a mistake."

As the two drivers emerge from a turn, Irvan's car shudders slightly. It drops back as Irvan's tire explodes, putting him out of the race. Jeff Gordon's rainbow car sails off. Two laps to go, and no one on Gordon's tail. Here comes the checkered flag—victory.

Chapter 6

Continued Success

Jeff Gordon is all about speed: His favorite animal is the cheetah because, he says, "I like fast, cool-looking cats." His favorite street car is the Ferrari Spider. His favorite color is red, because he likes the blur it creates at 200 miles per hour.

He loves race day. He lives for the moment when he straps on his helmet, climbs behind the wheel of his rainbow Chevy, and rolls onto the track before a screaming crowd of one hundred thousand fans. In the middle of that noisy, 180-mile-per-hour earthquake, Gordon feels most at home.

Sometimes he forgets to leave his work at the office. Recently Gordon was running late for a flight at the airport in Charlotte, North Carolina. Stepping on the gas in his black Chevy Camaro, he pushed it well over the speed limit. Soon a police officer pulled him over.

"I'm Jeff Gordon," racing's Golden Boy told the officer. "Do you follow racing?"

"Yes I do," replied the officer. "I'm a big Dale Earnhardt fan. Here's your ticket."

Jeff Gordon is all about religious faith: Part of staying on the right track, he believes, is putting everything in the right perspective. When he was a young, losses would leave

Jeff Gordon climbs out of his car after taking the pole for the NAPA 500 race at Atlanta Motor Speedway in November 2000.

him angry and frustrated. Then, one day, he attended a chapel service with fellow driver Lake Speed. The service moved him, Gordon said. It made him realize that many things in life are more important than winning or losing a car race.

"I don't pray about winning. I don't pray about making lots of money. I pray about forgiveness and about safety. And I pray for others. That side of things, I enjoy. I feel like I've been put on a platform to be able to display my beliefs in that."

Gordon does not push his religious beliefs on anyone, but he does not hide them. More than anything, he says, his faith in God gives him comfort when he is driving at high speeds. That is a time when he cannot allow fear to enter his mind.

Jeff Gordon is all about the fans: Unlike some superstar athletes—who become snobby with success—Gordon mingles with the fans every day. He patiently answers questions about the mechanics of his car. He attends dozens of charity events a year. He will be a guest speaker at any church that asks. Tennis superstar Monica Seles, a friend and fan, regards Gordon as the hardest-working athlete in sports. To Gordon, the explanation is simple: It is better to enjoy fame and success than to run away from it.

For that reason, he signs thousands and thousands of autographs. He gets many strange requests. "Some people want me to sign their arm or the top of their shoulder so they can get my name tattooed in," he said. "There are people with half of their backs that have number twenty-four and Rainbow colors and Jeff Gordon on it. I think, 'What happens if I change sponsors or numbers?'"

If Jeff Gordon can maintain his pace of recent years—ten wins per season—Gordon could break Richard Petty's record of 200 career Winston Cup victories by the age of

Fans pack the stands of the California Speedway in Fontana, California for the California 500 in May 1999. Jeff Gordon went on to win the race, his third first-place finish of the year.

forty-three. Ever since Petty hit the magic number 200 (at age forty-seven), most everyone in racing has believed the record was unbreakable. The NASCAR schedule used to feature fifty or sixty races a season. Some were at remote tracks against slim competition. These days there are about thirty-five races a year, and the good drivers show up every weekend.

Another reason is that no one in racing has ever been as dominant as Petty. At least not until Jeff Gordon showed up.

Would Gordon drive for another fifteen years? For now, he is not saying. He has hinted that he might slow down when he and his wife, Brooke, decide to have children. He wants to be around to help raise them. But, he also says, if he stays healthy and competitive, he would hate to retire from something he loves so much.

All those attitudes give a sense of what Jeff Gordon is about. They are one reason why he is regarded as NASCAR's version of Tiger Woods. He is someone who can bring new fans, from diverse backgrounds, into the audience. He is a young man who can be a poster boy for his sport in the twenty-first century.

How popular can he get? Petty—known as The King—was NASCAR's biggest-ever hero. But auto racing was not big across the country in Petty's day. There are many young sports fans who never even heard of him. Gordon may be able to combine Petty's great success on the track with the marketing success that athletes from other sports have had in recent years. Michael Jordan did it for basketball. Wayne Gretzky did it for hockey. Tiger Woods is now doing it for golf. Can Jeff Gordon do it for auto racing?

Certainly his all-American looks are attracting new followers to this traditionally male-oriented, blue-collar sport. Gordon has his own popular Web site and a twenty-thousand-member fan club. David Letterman has invited

Gordon (24) flies past Robert Pressley (77) during the Food City 500 in Bristol, Tennessee on March 25, 2001.

Gordon onto *The Late Show* at least five times. Once Letterman set up a race through the streets of Manhattan between Gordon and New York City taxi drivers. Gordon glided past the cabbies like he glides past his NASCAR rivals.

Gordon's boyish good looks make him a favorite of women. "My mother-in-law is eighty-three and she's become his greatest fan," said John Krol, chief executive officer of DuPont, Gordon's main sponsor. "She's never even had a driver's license, and now she watches every race. It's incredible."

He also has great appeal among racing's youngest fans. All over the country, said Charlotte Motor Speedway promoter H. A. "Humpy" Wheeler, parents are putting their five-year-olds in quarter-midget race cars so the kids can be like Gordon.

Gordon takes his relationship with fans—especially children—quite seriously. In addition to giving his all each weekend, he avoids behavior that might embarrass himself, his family, or his sport. In recent years, some athletes have insisted they are not role models. For instance, basketball superstar Charles Barkley said that children should look to their parents—not to him—for guidance.

Gordon agrees that parents should be the top role models. But he still believes that athletes can play a positive role in a youngster's life:

> Kids look up to athletes and anybody who's on TV a lot. I certainly take that as a compliment as being a role model. I don't try to be someone I'm not. I try to be myself. I try to be really good to the kids, because that was me when I was five years old. As a kid, I loved [former driver] Rick Mears. He was a big influence to me. He seemed like a really good guy and a great race car driver. He didn't ever swear. He was just a good guy.

I grew up following him and later I got to meet him. That went a long way with me.

Nothing will help Gordon reach people more than continued success. He slumped a bit in 1999, surrendering his Winston Cup points title to Dale Jarrett. Still, Gordon finished a respectable sixth. He won 7 races, and took home another $5.8 million in earnings. Not too shabby for a supposedly sub-par season.

He opened the 1999 season with a thrilling win in the Daytona 500, stockcar racing's biggest event. Gordon hung with the pack of leaders through most of the race. With just ten laps to go, he decided to make his move. Going around Turn 1, he dove his car underneath leader Rusty Wallace and nearly into the lapped car being driven by Ricky Rudd. It was the kind of daring move that fans love—and some other drivers hate. Wallace angrily shook his fist as Gordon sped by.

With eight laps to go, Gordon had a lead. But his top rival, Dale Earnhardt, quickly pulled up to his rear bumper. Two years earlier, a Gordon-Earnhardt battle ended with the two bumping each other while they were side by side, and Earnhardt's car eventually rolled over as Gordon cruised on to win. This time Earnhardt did not make it alongside Gordon. Pressing his foot to the floor, Gordon pushed the most he could out of his No. 24 car. For twenty miles, a charging, weaving, snarling Earnhardt stayed on his tail. But for twenty miles, Gordon kept the lead. He won the race, and the huge $1.1 million prize that went with it. Gordon and Earnhardt's rivalry came to a tragic end in 2001 when Earnhardt was killed in a crash during the Daytona 500.

There really are two sides to Jeff Gordon. Outside his race car, he is warm, gracious, and engaging. But strap him into a 3,400-pound stock car, flip a few toggle switches, and

Jeff Gordon's religious faith helps him keep things in perspective. It is also a comfort to him when he's driving high speeds.

wave a green flag, and an entirely different side of Jeff Gordon takes over.

"Out of the car, he's like a junior high school kid," says fellow driver Kyle Petty. "But inside the car, he's a fierce competitor. Whatever it takes to win, that's what he does."

That is what Jeff Gordon plans to keep doing for years to come.

Career Statistics

Season	Races Started	Wins	Top 5s	Top 10s	Poles	Earnings	Winston Cup Standings
1992	1	0	0	0	0	$6,285	N/A
1993	30	0	7	11	1	$765,168	14
1994	31	2	7	14	1	$1,779,523	8
1995	31	7	17	23	8	$4,347,343	1
1996	31	10	21	24	5	$3,428,485	2
1997	32	10	22	23	1	$6,375,658	1
1998	33	13	26	28	7	$9,306,584	1
1999	34	7	18	21	8	$5,858,633	6
2000	34	3	11	22	2	$2,588,455	9
Totals	257	52	129	166	33	$34,456,134	3 Titles

Where to Write Jeff Gordon

Mr. Jeff Gordon
c/o National Association for Stock Car Auto Racing (NASCAR)
1801 W. International Speedway Blvd.
Daytona Beach, FL 32114-1243

On the Internet at:

http://www.jeffgordon.com
http://rpm.espn.go.com/rpm/driver?series=wc&id=jgordon
http://www.nascar.com/DRIVERS/winston/JGordon00/index.html

Index